Doctors
In Our Community

Erin Heath

PowerKiDS
press.

New York

To Sasha. May she be walking in front of someone's book somewhere.

Published in 2010 by The Rosen Publishing Group, Inc.
29 East 21st Street, New York, NY 10010

First Edition

Editor: Nicole Pristash
Book Design: Greg Tucker
Photo Researcher: Jessica Gerweck

Photo Credits: Cover Thomas Barwick/Getty Images; pp. 5, 23, 24 (center), 24 (center-right) Shutterstock.com; p. 7 Ron Levine/Getty Images; p. 9 LWA/Getty Images; p. 11 Hans Neleman/Getty Images; pp. 13, 24 (right) Jochen Sands/Getty Images; p. 15 © www.iStockphoto.com/Joel Blit; p. 17 © www.iStockphoto.com/Andrei Malov; pp. 19, 24 (center-left) © www.iStockphoto.com/Valerijs Vinogradovs; p. 21 Shannon Fagon/Getty Images; p. 24 (left) www.iStockphoto.com/Matthew Rambo.

Library of Congress Cataloging-in-Publication Data

Heath, Erin.
  Doctors in our community / Erin Heath. — 1st ed.
     p. cm. — (On the job)
  Includes index.
  ISBN 978-1-4042-8070-0 (lib. bdg.) — ISBN 978-1-4358-2454-6 (pbk.) — ISBN 978-1-4358-2462-1 (6-pack)
  1. Physicians—Juvenile literature. I. Title.
  R690.H4357 2010
  610.92—dc22

                              2008049467

Manufactured in the United States of America

Contents

Doctors help people who are hurt or sick. Their jobs keep them very busy.

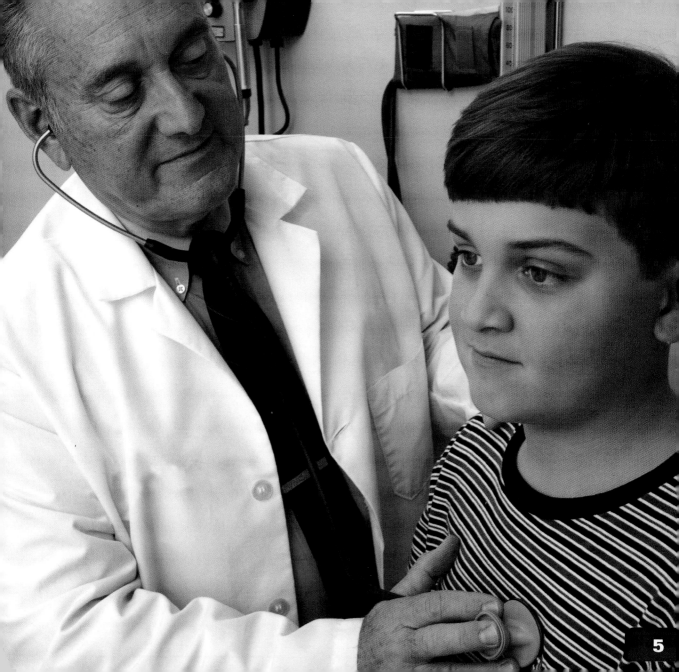

When it is time for a checkup or a shot, you visit a family doctor.

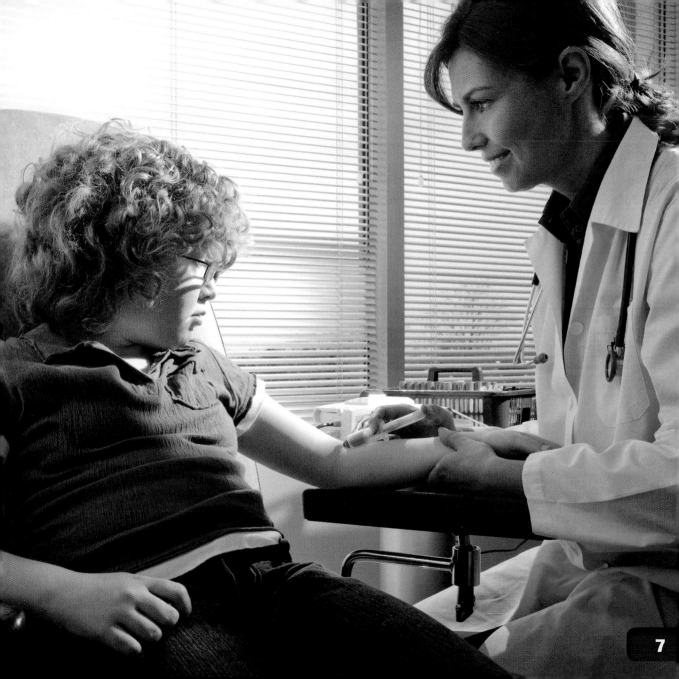

A family doctor checks to see how tall you have grown.

Some doctors work in big **hospitals**, and some doctors work in small offices.

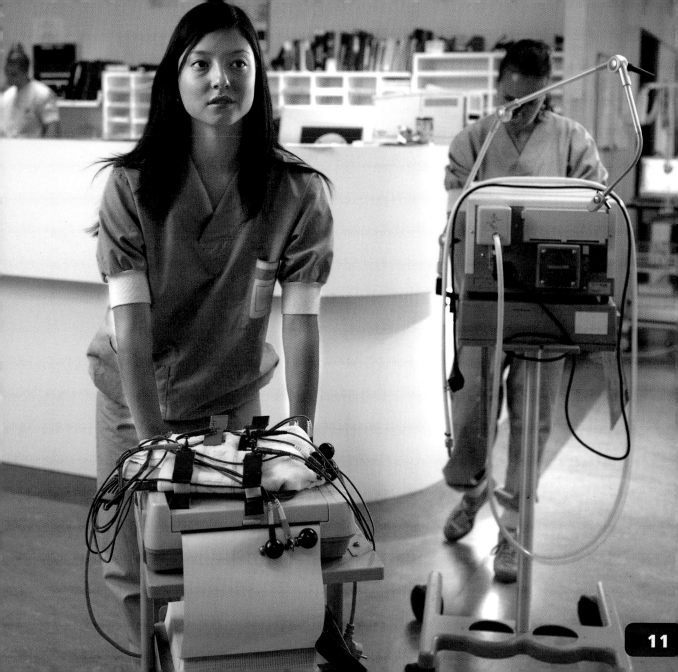

These doctors are **surgeons**. Surgeons sometimes **operate** on people who are very sick.

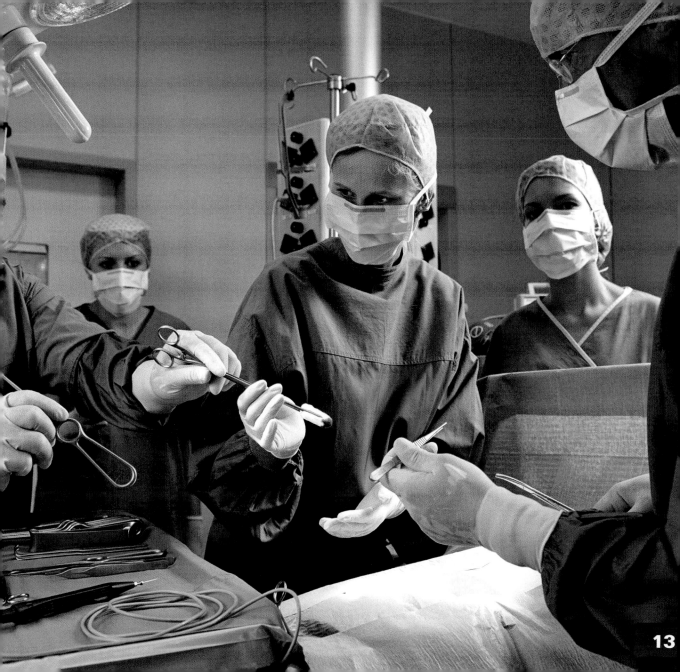

Surgeons do their work in operating rooms.

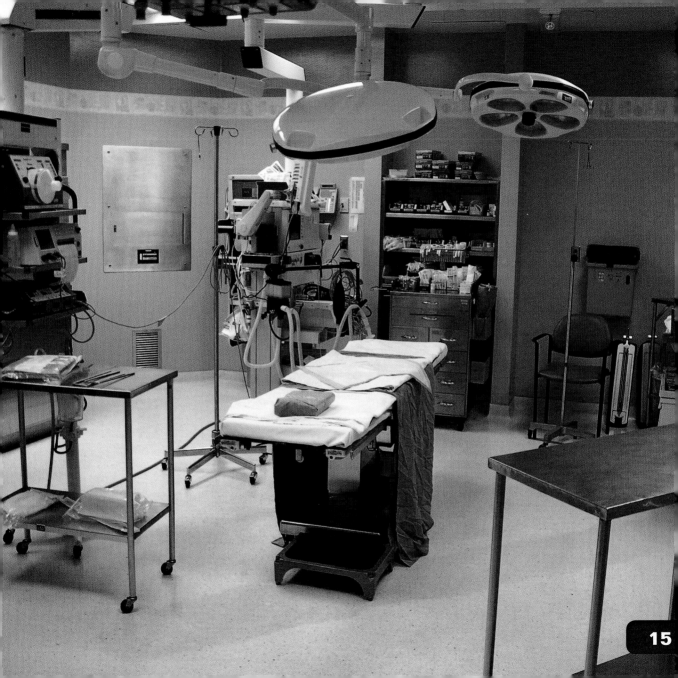

Surgeons wear **masks** while they work.

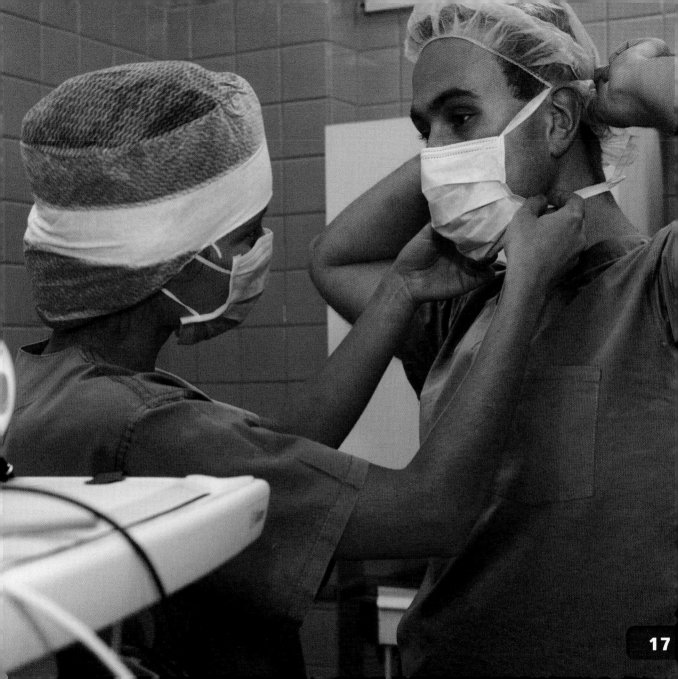

Doctors use many machines and tools every day. This machine keeps track of the **patient**'s heartbeat.

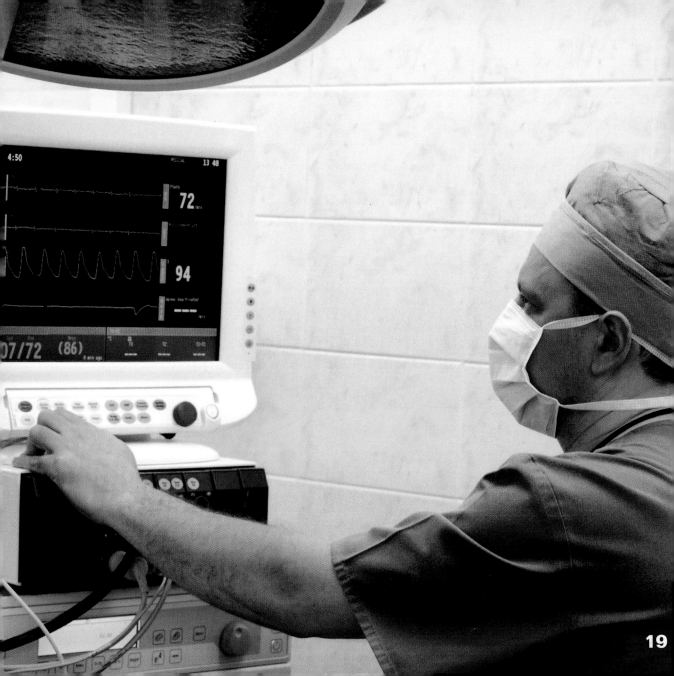

Doctors talk to their patients to help find out what is making them feel sick.

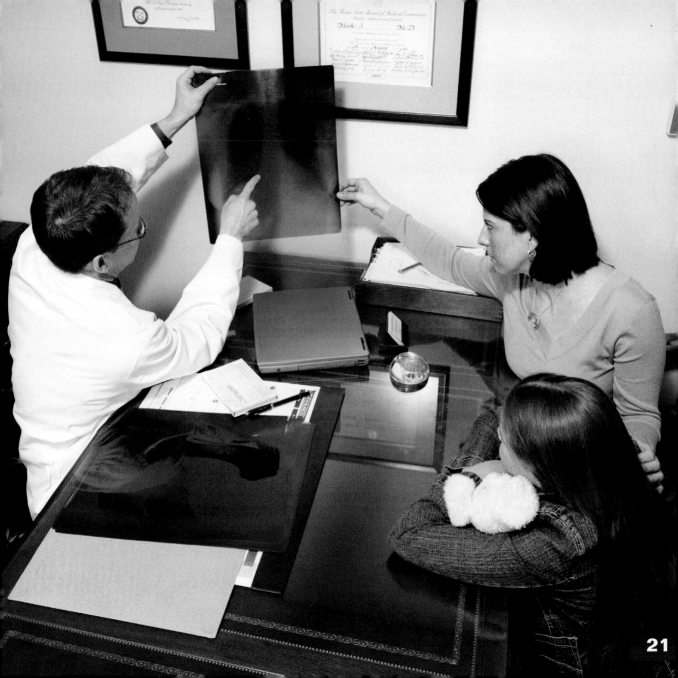

Doctors work hard to help us feel better.

Words to Know

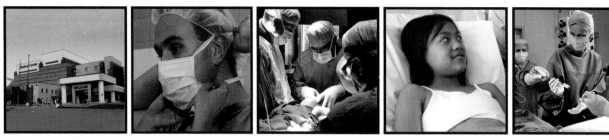

hospital   mask   operate   patient   surgeons

Index

Web Sites

Due to the changing nature of Internet links, PowerKids Press has developed an online list of Web sites related to the subject of this book. This site is updated regularly. Please use this link to access the list:

www.powerkidslinks.com/job/doctor/

24